IT'S TIME TO EAT CRAN-APPLE SAUCE

It's Time to Eat CRAN-APPLE SAUCE

Walter the Educator

Silent King Books
A WhichHead Entertainment Imprint

Copyright © 2024 by Walter the Educator

All rights reserved. No part of this book may be reproduced in any manner whatsoever without written per- mission except in the case of brief quotations embodied in critical articles and reviews.

First Printing, 2024

Disclaimer

This book is a literary work; the story is not about specific persons, locations, situations, and/or circumstances unless mentioned in a historical context. Any resemblance to real persons, locations, situations, and/or circumstances is coincidental. This book is for entertainment and informational purposes only. The author and publisher offer this information without warranties expressed or implied. No matter the grounds, neither the author nor the publisher will be accountable for any losses, injuries, or other damages caused by the reader's use of this book. The use of this book acknowledges an understanding and acceptance of this disclaimer.

It's Time to Eat CRAN-APPLE SAUCE is a collectible early learning book by Walter the Educator suitable for all ages belonging to Walter the Educator's Time to Eat Book Series. Collect more books at WaltertheEducator.com

USE THE EXTRA SPACE TO TAKE NOTES AND DOCUMENT YOUR MEMORIES

CRAN-APPLE SAUCE

It's time to eat, come gather near,

It's Time to Eat
Cran-Apple Sauce

A special dish that brings us cheer.

Sweet and tangy, red and bright,

Cran-Apple Sauce is such delight!

Apples chopped and cranberries round,

Cooking together with a bubbling sound.

A sprinkle of sugar, a dash of spice,

The smell alone is oh so nice!

The cranberries pop, the apples stew,

The pot turns red, a magical hue.

Stir it up, it's almost done,

Cran-Apple Sauce is so much fun!

Spoon it out and take a peek,

It's smooth and shiny, warm and sleek.

On your plate or in a bowl,

Cran-Apple Sauce will make you whole!

It's Time to Eat
Cran-Apple Sauce

A little tart, a little sweet,

The perfect combo in every treat.

Try it with turkey, or on some bread,

This yummy sauce will fill your head!

Share it with friends, pass it around,

Happiness grows with every sound.

A cheerful laugh, a tasty bite,

Cran-Apple Sauce feels just right!

It's good for lunch, or dinner too,

Or as a snack, it's up to you!

Healthy and yummy, smooth and bold,

A treasure of flavors to behold.

When the bowl is empty and clean,

We'll dream of sauce in shades of sheen.

Tomorrow we'll make another batch,

It's Time to Eat
Cran-Apple Sauce

Cran-Apple Sauce is hard to match!

So grab a spoon, don't wait too long,

Join in the Cran-Apple song.

It's time to eat, hooray, hooray,

Cran-Apple Sauce has made our day!

Let's thank the fruits, so fresh and fine,

For making sauce that's so divine.

Cranberries red, apples so sweet,

It's Time to Eat Cran-Apple Sauce

Together they make the perfect treat!

ABOUT THE CREATOR

Walter the Educator is one of the pseudonyms for Walter Anderson. Formally educated in Chemistry, Business, and Education, he is an educator, an author, a diverse entrepreneur, and he is the son of a disabled war veteran. "Walter the Educator" shares his time between educating and creating. He holds interests and owns several creative projects that entertain, enlighten, enhance, and educate, hoping to inspire and motivate you. Follow, find new works, and stay up to date with Walter the Educator™

at WaltertheEducator.com

www.ingramcontent.com/pod-product-compliance
Lightning Source LLC
LaVergne TN
LVHW052011060526
838201LV00059B/3975